N

Cuisine

Amrita Patel

New Dawn

NEW DAWN
a division of Sterling Publishers (P) Ltd.
A-59, Okhla Industrial Area, Phase-II, New Delhi-110020
Tel: 26387070, 26386209
Fax: 91-11-26383788
E-mail: ghai@nde.vsnl.net.in
www.sterlingpublishers.com

Mughlai Cuisine
© 2004, Sterling Publishers (P) Ltd.
ISBN: 81 207 2646 4

Published by Sterling Publishers Pvt. Ltd., New Delhi-110020.
Lasertypeset by Vikas Compographics, New Delhi-110020.
Printed at Sai Early Learners Pvt. Ltd., New Delhi-110020.

Contents

Contents

Preface

Mughlai cooking has occupied a very important place in every Indian household. Though it is a legacy of the Mughals, Mughlai cooking is a part of almost all Indian festivals and celebrations.

Mughlai cuisine stands apart as the empress of the Indian range of cooking. It lays stress on good ingredients, low flame and rich spices. Another important aspect of this type of cuisine is that the use of spices in the meat dishes brings out the flavour of the meat. Goat meat is generally used in most of the meat dishes, though chicken biryani is a delicacy too.

The vegetarian Mughlai dishes do not require heavy flavouring and are cooked in such a way that the vegetables retain their crunchiness. One of the great specialities of Mughlai cooking and a very popular one too is kababs. These serve as snacks as well as meal accompaniments.

This book lists out the recipes in different sections for easy reference. The method used is easy and simple to follow.

The book will be a handy guide for novices as well as experienced cooks.

Glossary

VEGETABLES

Aubergine/Brinjal	*Baingan*
Bittergourd	*Karela*
Cabbage	*Patta gobi*
Capsicum	*Shimla mirch*
Carrot	*Gajar*
Cauliflower	*Phool gobi*
Cucumber	*Kheera*
Green chillies	*Hari mirch*
Ladiesfinger	*Bhindi*
Lemon	*Nimbu*
Lotus stem	*Kamal kakri*
Peas	*Matar*
Potato	*Aloo*
Spinach	*Palak*
Onion	*Piaz*
Tomato	*Tamatar*
Yam	*Zamikand*

FRUITS and DRY FRUITS

Almonds	*Badam*
Apple	*Seb*
Apricots	*Khurmani*
Cashew nuts	*Kaju*
Coconut	*Narial*
Dates	*Khajur*
Grapes	*Angur*
Groundnuts	*Moongphali*

Mango	Aam
Orange	Santra
Pineapple	Ananas
Pistachio	Pista
Pomegranate seeds	Anardana
Puffed lotus seeds	Makhana
Raisins	Kishmish

HERBS, GREENS AND SPICES

Aniseed	Saunf
Asafoetida	Hing
Bay leaf	Tej patta
Black cardamom	Bara elaichi
Black pepper	Kali mirch
Caraway seeds	Ajwain
Cardamom	Elaichi
Cinnamon	Dalchini
Cloves	Laung
Coriander leaves	Dhania
Cumin seeds	Jeera
Curry leaves	Curry patta
Dried ginger	Sonth
Fenugreek	Methi
Garlic	Lasun
Garam masala	Mixture of powdered peppercorns, cloves, cinnamon and cardamom
Ginger	Adrakh
Mace	Javetri
Mango powder	Amchur

7

Mint	Pudina
Mustard seeds	Rai or sarson
Nutmeg	Jaiphal
Peppercorns	Sabut kali mirch
Poppy seeds	Khus khus
Red chilli	Lal mirch
Saffron	Kesar
Sesame seeds	Til
Tamarind	Imli
Turmeric powder	Haldi
White cumin seeds	Shahjeera

LENTILS

Bengal gram	Chana dal
Black gram	Urad sabut
Chickpeas	Kabuli chana
Green gram	Mung sabut
Red split lentils	Masoor dal

MISCELLANEOUS

Clarified butter	Ghee
Cottage cheese	Paneer
Flour	Maida
Minced meat	Keema
Silver foil	Chandi ka vark
Soda bicarb	Meetha soda
Solidified milk	Khoya
Vinegar	Sirka
Wheat flour	Atta
Yeast	Khameer

8

Breads

Aloo Paratha

Serves 8

Ingredients

For the dough
500 gm wheat flour
A pinch of salt
Water or milk
½ cup ghee

For the filling
250 gm potatoes, mashed
1 tsp cumin seeds
A few coriander leaves, chopped
Salt and pepper to taste

10

Method

1. Place the flour and salt in a bowl. Add enough water or milk to make a firm dough.

2. Divide the dough into 8 portions and roll out each into a circle.

3. Mix the mashed potatoes with the rest of the ingredients for the filling.

4. Spread the filling evenly over the dough circles. Fold the edges around the filling, roll into a ball and then flatten it into a circular shape, about 6 inches in diameter.

5. Pour a little ghee, into a heavy-bottomed frying pan and cook each paratha on both sides, over a low flame, till crisp and golden brown. Apply the ghee on both sides while browning. Serve hot.

Naan

Serves 8

Ingredients

250 gm flour
½ tsp salt
125 ml milk
1 tsp sugar
30 gm yeast
¼ cup butter
½ tsp baking powder
1 tbsp poppy seeds

Method

1. In a large mixing bowl, sift together the flour, baking powder, salt and sugar.

2. Blend the yeast with 2 tbsp of milk. Warm the remaining milk and add to the yeast with 1½ tbsp of butter. Mix well.

3. Make a hollow in the centre of the flour and gradually pour the yeast mixture. Knead well until the dough is smooth.

4. Cover with a cloth and leave to rise for about 2 hours at room temperature.

5. Divide the dough into 8 portions and form each into a ball with greased hands. Cover the dough balls with a cloth and leave for about 15 minutes.

6. Flatten each ball into a circle of about 5 inches in diameter. Brush the tops with the melted butter and sprinkle with the poppy seeds.

7. Place the dough circles on a greased baking tray and bake at 230° C for about 10 minutes, or until the naan is puffed up. Serve hot.

Piaz Ki Roti

Serves 8

Ingredients

500 gm wheat flour
A pinch of soda bicarbonate
3 onions, finely chopped
A sprig of curry leaves, finely chopped
6 green chillies, finely chopped
1 tbsp coarsely chopped coriander leaves
Ghee
Salt to taste

Method

1. Add the chopped ingredients to the wheat flour.

2. Add a pinch of soda bicarbonate, salt and enough water to make a thick batter of pouring consistency.

3. Heat a frying pan and then lightly grease it. Pour enough batter to cover it thinly.

4. Pour a little ghee around the edges. Flip and brown both the sides. Serve hot.

Chana Dal Paratha

Serves 8

Ingredients

500 gm flour
½ tsp ground cardamoms
500 gm Bengal gram
3 cloves
500 gm sugar
2 tsp sesame oil
3 tbsp butter

Method

1. Sieve the flour, add the oil and enough water to make a thick dough. Roll into medium-sized balls, flatten them and keep aside.

2. Boil the Bengal gram in 2 cups of water until tender.

3. Drain off the water and add the sugar, cardamoms and cloves and stir till a thread-like syrup is formed.

4. Blend this mixture in a blender to form a paste.

5. Fill the flattened balls, which were kept aside, with the gram mixture. Close the edges tightly and roll out into a round pancake.

6. Roast on a hot griddle till crisp and golden brown. Dot with the butter and serve hot.

Gobi Paratha

Serves 8

Ingredients

500 gm wheat flour
1½" piece of ginger, finely chopped
500 gm cauliflower, grated
1 tbsp finely chopped coriander leaves
2 onions, finely chopped
1 tsp garam masala
2 green chillies, finely chopped
Ghee
1 tbsp dried pomegranate seeds, crushed
Salt to taste

Method

1. Grate the cauliflower coarsely. Sprinkle with salt. Keep aside for 30 minutes.
2. Squeeze out the water and mix the cauliflower with the finely chopped onions, ginger, coriander leaves, chillies crushed pomegranate seeds and garam masala.
3. Sieve the flour, add 2 tbsp of ghee, salt and enough water to make a stiff dough.
4. Divide into 6 portions and roll into thick round circles. Place a little of the cauliflower mixture in the centre, seal the edges.
5. Form into a ball and then roll out as thin as possible without letting the stuffing break through.
6. Heat a frying pan and roast these parathas on both sides, adding a little ghee, till evenly browned.

Keema Tandoori Roti

Serves 4-6

Ingredients

375 gm wheat flour
1 tsp salt
2 tbsp yeast
125 gm minced meat, parboiled
Salt to taste

Method

1. Mix the flour, yeast and salt with enough water to form a stiff dough.

2. Cover with a cotton cloth and keep aside for 2-3 hours till the dough rises.

3. Knead the meat with a little salt into the dough.

4. Divide into equal portions and make flat round cakes with the help of the palm.

5. Bake in a tandoor or a barbecue.

6. Serve hot with chutney or any dip.

Puri

Serves 6-8

Ingredients

2 glasses whole wheat flour
1 tsp salt
1 tsp cumin seeds
250 gm potatoes, boiled
Water
Oil for frying

Method

1. Sieve the flour. Add 1 tsp each of salt and cumin seeds to the flour.

2. Peel the boiled potatoes.

3. Knead the potatoes into the flour till dry. Add a little water if necessary to make a stiff dough. Cover with a damp cloth and keep aside for half an hour.

4. Knead the dough once more and make lemon-sized balls. You can roll out the puris, about 4" in diameter and keep them aside.

5. Heat the oil in a wok till smoking hot. Slide in a puri gently and stroke till it puffs up. Turn it over. Lightly brown both sides. Drain.

6. Repeat with the remaining balls of the dough.

Keema Paratha

Serves 8

Ingredients

500 gm wheat flour
225 gm minced meat
1 tsp coriander powder
½ tsp red chilli powder
1 onion, finely chopped
1 tsp garam masala
Ghee
Salt to taste

Method

1. Parboil the minced meat and keep aside.

2. Heat 2 tbsp ghee and lightly fry the chopped onions.

3. Add the coriander powder, red chilli powder, garam masala and salt. Fry till brown.

4. Add 2 tbsp of water and simmer till the mixture is tender and dry. Mix the meat well with this.

5. Sieve the flour with salt, rub a little ghee and add enough water to make a soft dough.

6. Divide into 16 portions and roll out each portion into a thin circle.

7. Spread a little of the meat mixture on one circle and place another rolled out circle on top.

8. Fold the edges of both the circles together.

9. Heat a little ghee in a frying pan.

10. Roast the stuffed parathas on both sides till crisp and golden brown.

11. Serve with chutney.

Rice Treats

Chicken Biryani

Ingredients

1 ½ kg chicken
250 gm basmati rice, soaked in water
for 30 minutes
1 large onion, thinly sliced
2 tomatoes, sliced
2 hard-boiled eggs, sliced (opt.)
1 tbsp garam masala
5 tbsp curd
150 ml water
Salt to taste

Method

1. Wash, skin and cut the chicken into medium-size pieces.
2. Saute the sliced onion in a large pan. Sprinkle the garam masala and salt. Add the chicken pieces and water.
3. Bring to the boil, cover and simmer until the chicken is tender and cooked.
4. Remove the chicken pieces from the stock and mix in the curd. Boil this stock until it is reduced by one-third. Pour this over the chicken pieces.
5. Drain the rice and partially cook in 600 ml of boiling salted water for four minutes. Drain the starch water thoroughly.
6. Spread the partially-cooked rice over the chicken mixture. Cook in a moderate oven at 180° C for 30-40 minutes. Serve hot, garnished with the sliced tomatoes and hard-boiled eggs.

Kesari Chawal

Ingredients

500 gm basmati rice
1 medium onion, sliced
1 small pod of garlic, crushed
1 tsp salt
100 gm ghee
1 tsp tumeric powder
1 tsp cumin seeds
½ tsp saffron soaked in 1 tbsp hot water
1 l water

Method

1. Wash the rice well.
2. Heat the ghee in a heavy saucepan. Fry the sliced onions till they are soft.
3. Add the garlic, turmeric powder and cumin seeds and mix well.
4. Add the rice and stir well. Add the saffron along with the water.
5. Then add the water and salt, cover and simmer till the rice is done.
6. Serve hot.

Pulao

Serves 6

Ingredients

*500 gm basmati rice, cleaned and
washed
1 medium onion, finely sliced
170 gm ghee
10 cloves
1 l water
3" piece of cinnamon
10 cardamoms
100 gm raisins
50 gm almonds, blanched
Salt to taste*

Method

1. Heat the ghee in a heavy saucepan and fry the sliced onions till soft.

2. Add the cloves, cinnamon, cardamoms and fry for a minute.

3. Add the washed rice. Fry well over a low flame.

4. Add salt and cover the rice with the water. Bring to the boil and then simmer with the lid closed, till the rice is done and the water has been absorbed.

5. Before serving, fry the raisins and almonds in a little oil and mix into the rice. Garnish with bits of silver foil.

Prawn Pulao

Serves 6

Ingredients

500 gm basmati rice, cleaned and
washed
500 gm prawns, cleaned and deveined
1 large onion, finely sliced
3 flakes of garlic, chopped
¼ cup desiccated coconut
1 cup peas
1 tbsp tamarind juice
1 egg, 1 l water
4 cloves
6 peppercorns
1" piece cinnamon
1 tsp red chilli powder
1 tsp tumeric powder
2 tbsp ghee
Salt to taste

Method

1. Mix the peas, prawns, tamarind juice, chilli-turmeric powder and keep aside for ½ an hour.

2. Heat 1tbsp ghee in a large saucepan and fry the onion, garlic and coconut till light brown in colour.

3. Add the cloves, peppercorns and cinnamon and fry for 2 minutes.

4. Add the rice and fry till dry. Add the water and sprinkle with salt. Cook till nearly done.

5. Heat the remaining ghee and fry the prawn mixture. Cook till the prawns are tender.

6. Add the prawn mixture to the rice, stir gently and leave to cook. Serve hot, garnished with the coriander leaves.

Vegetable Biryani

Serves 4

Ingredients

225 gm basmati rice
4 onions, finely sliced
½ kg of mixed vegetables
1 bay leaf, 5 tbsp ghee
½ tsp each of shahjeera and red chilli
powder
2 tbsp each of coriander and mint
leaves, chopped
50 gm cashew nuts, fried
1" piece of ginger, 30 gm raisins
8 flakes of garlic
4 each of green chillies, cloves and
cardamoms
2 tsp coriander powder
2" piece of cinnamon
Salt to taste

Method

1. Wash, clean and soak the rice for 15 minutes.

2. Heat the ghee, add the shahjeera and bay leaf.

3. Add the sliced onion and fry till light brown.

4. Add the spices and fry for 2 minutes.

5. Add the mint and coriander leaves.

6. Drain the rice well and add to the pan. Fry well.

7. Add the mixed vegetables and stir the mixture.

8. Add little more than double the amount of water. Bring to the boil, then lower the flame and simmer till the rice is done.

9. Garnish with the cashew nuts and raisins.

Dilkhush Pulao

Ingredients

250 gm basmati rice
4 onions, sliced
1 cup fresh orange juice
2 slices of pineapple
4 cloves
2" piece of cinnamon
4 cardamoms
1 tsp red chilli powder
½ apple, diced
2 tbsp seedless grapes
50 gm almonds, pista and cashew nuts
4 tbsp ghee
½ l water
Salt to taste

Method

1. Clean the rice and soak in water for 15 minutes.

2. Pour the ghee in a deep vessel and fry the onions.

3. When the onions are brown, add the red chilli powder. Then add the cloves, cinnamon and cardamom.

4. Drain the rice thoroughly and add it to the above mixture. Fry well.

5. Stir the orange juice in ½ l water and pour over the rice. Bring it to the boil and then lower the flame. Let it simmer.

6. When the rice is semi-cooked, add the diced apple, pineapple, grapes and nuts. Cook till done. Serve hot.

Fish Pulao

Serves 4

Ingredients

350 gm basmati rice (soaked for 1 hour)
1 large fish (cleaned and cut into pieces)
3 large onions, sliced
½ each of lemon and coconut
5 tbsp of ghee
Salt to taste

Grind to paste

1 tsp coriander seeds, roasted
2 dry red chillies
1 tsp cumin seeds
½ tsp turmeric powder
4 cloves
60 gm desiccated coconut
1" piece of ginger
A bunch of coriander leaves

40

Method

1. Grate the coconut and boil it in 1 cup water for 15 minutes. Stain the mixture and keep the coconut milk aside.

2. Heat 3 tbsp ghee in a pan and fry the ground masala till it becomes slightly red in colour.

3. Add the fish pieces and salt and cook till tender.

4. Heat 2 tbsp ghee in a wok, and fry the onions till brown.

5. Add the drained rice, salt and mix well.

6. Pour in the fish gravy, coconut milk, lemon juice and cook over a medium flame till the rice is almost cooked.

7. Arrange all the fish pieces on top, cover and cook over a low flame for 10 more minutes. Serve hot.

Mango Pulao

Ingredients

725 gm basmati rice
3 medium-sized green mangoes
1 ½ cups grated coconut
1 tbsp black gram or
whole green gram
300 ml ghee
1 tsp mustard seeds
1 tsp cumin seeds
A little turmeric powder
A few curry leaves
A few green chillies
Salt to taste

Method

1. Boil water in a container. Clean the rice and put it into the boiling water. When it is three-quarters cooked, remove from the fire and drain the excess water.

2. When the rice cools, add the turmeric powder and half the ghee. Mix well.

3. Peel, cut and grate the mangoes.

4. Grind the cumin seeds, half the green chillies and grated coconut.

5. Mix it with the grated mango and then add to the rice.

6. Heat the remaining oil in a pan and add the mustard seeds. When they begin to splutter, add the black gram, curry leaves and the remaining chillies.

7. Add this to the rice and stir well. Serve hot.

Rice with Meatballs

Serves 4

Ingredients

1 glass basmati rice
½ kg minced meat
2 large onions
½ tbsp ginger-garlic paste
½ tbsp poppy seeds
½ cup curd
½ cup oil
½ tbsp blanched almonds
1 tbsp garam masala
Salt to taste

Method

1. Add salt to the minced meat. Wash and squeeze out all the water.

2. Grind the spices and also the almonds.

3. Peel and cut one onion, grind with the minced meat. Keep aside. Slice the other onion.

4. Heat the oil and fry the sliced onion. Add the curd. Cook over a low flame.

5. Form meatballs out of the minced meat mixture and put them in the curd gravy. Keep stirring to avoid scorching. Add the garam masala. Stir.

6. Parboil the rice and drain.

7. In a large pot, spread a layer of rice. Alternate with a layer of meat balls. Keep layering till all is used. Cook over a high flame for 2 minutes, lower the flame and cook for 5 minutes more.

Gosht Pulao

Ingredients

750 gm boned lamb
225 gm basmati rice, soaked in water
for 30 minutes
2 large onions, finely sliced
3 flakes of garlic, sliced
300 ml curd
1 lemon
170 gm ghee
4 tsp coriander powder
4 tsp cumin powder
4 cardamoms
1 bay leaf
50 gm raisins
50 gm almonds, blanched

Method

1. Cut the lamb into chunks, removing any fat.

2. Heat 100 grams ghee in a large saucepan and fry the lamb pieces till lightly browned. Remove from the pan and keep aside.

3. Fry the sliced onions and garlic in the same oil till the onions turn translucent.

4. Add the coriander powder, cumin powder, cardamoms and bay leaf and fry for one minute more.

5. Squeeze the juice of the lemon and pour it into the pan. Then add the curd.

6. Toss in the lamb pieces, cover and cook for 20 minutes.

7. Drain the water from the rice.

8. Heat the remaining ghee in a separate pan and add the rice.

9. Fry well and add double the amount of water (including the gravy of the lamb) and cook for 10 minutes.

10. Add the lamb, mix well, cover and cook till the rice is done.

11. Add the raisins and almonds, stirring gently.

12. Serve hot.

Eggetarian Surprises

Malai Masaledaar Ande

Ingredients

6 eggs, hard-boiled
½ tsp garam masala
300 ml milk
2 tbsp ghee
2 medium-sized onions
1" piece of ginger
A few coriander leaves,
coarsely chopped
4 green chillies
Salt to taste

Method

1. Shell the eggs and halve lengthwise.

2. Grind the onions, ginger and green chillies to a paste.

3. Heat the ghee in a saucepan and fry the paste for a minute.

4. Put in the eggs and fry till the masala turns pale brown.

5. Add the milk and salt.

6. When the milk begins to boil, add the chopped coriander leaves and simmer till the gravy thickens.

7. Before serving, sprinkle with the garam masala.

Ande Ka Korma

Ingredients

6 eggs, separated
2 tbsp cashew nuts, coarsely chopped
6 medium onions, finely chopped
3 tbsp ghee
150 ml milk
Salt to taste

Grind to paste

8 green chillies
6 cloves
1 tbsp grated coconut
1" piece of cinnamon
3 tbsp coriander powder
2 cardamoms
½ tsp turmeric powder
1" piece of ginger

Method

1. Beat the egg whites till stiff.

2. Add the egg yolks, milk and salt. Beat the mixture for 10 minutes.

3. Place the bowl with the egg mixture in a larger vessel containing a little water. Double boil till the egg mixture is set.

4. Take out the set egg mixture and cut into cubes.

5. Heat the ghee in a heavy saucepan and fry the cashew nuts till golden brown. Add all the ingredients ground to a paste. Cook well over a low flame.

6. Add 300 ml warm water and bring it to the boil.

7. Add the egg cubes and cook over a low flame till the gravy thickens. Serve hot.

Eggs with Tomato and Capsicum

Serves 4

Ingredients

4 eggs, beaten
1 large tomato, blanched and chopped
1 large onion, finely chopped
1 capsicum, finely chopped
4 tbsp oil
A few sprigs of mint and coriander,
chopped
2 green chillies, finely chopped
Salt to taste

Method

1. Heat the oil. Fry the chopped onions.

2. While they are browning, add the capsicum and tomato.

3. Add the coriander-mint leaves, green chillies and salt to the eggs.

4. Pour it over the onion-tomato mixture.

5. Quickly stir it and let it cook over a high flame.

6. Remove from the fire and serve hot.

Andon Ka Salan

Ingredients

6 eggs, hard-boiled
250 gm onion, finely chopped
1 large tomato, blanched and chopped
2 tbsp ginger-garlic paste
2 tbsp oil
1 tsp red chilli powder
½ tsp turmeric
2 tbsp fresh cream
Salt to taste

Method

1. Shell and halve the hard-boiled eggs.

2. Heat the oil and fry the onions till golden brown.

3. Add the ginger-garlic paste and fry for a couple of minutes.

4. Add the chopped tomato, chilli powder, turmeric and salt. Stir till the oil floats on top.

5. Add the halved eggs to the gravy and carefully stir for a few minutes before taking them off the fire.

Ande Nargisi Kofte

Serves 4

Ingredients

4 eggs, hard-boiled
1 green chilli, finely chopped
1-2 slices of bread
1 small onion, finely chopped
1 tbsp ghee
Salt to taste

For the tomato sauce

500 gm tomatoes, peeled
½ tsp garam masala
1 tbsp chopped coriander leaves
1 tsp red chilli powder
Salt and pepper to taste

Method

1. Shell and halve the eggs lengthwise. Carefully remove the yolks and keep aside.

2. Crumble the bread slices and soak in cold water.

3. When soft, squeeze and drain the water. Mash well.

4. Mash the egg yolks and add to the mashed bread.

5. Add a tbsp of the ghee.

6. Add the chopped onion, green chilli and salt and mix well.

7. Spoon in this mixture into the egg whites.

8. To prepare the tomato sauce mix all the ingredients for it and simmer till tender.

9. Place the stuffed egg whites in a flat ovenproof dish.

10. Pour the tomato sauce over the egg whites.

11. Cover the dish with an aluminium foil and bake in an oven at 180°C, till the sauce simmers.

12. Remove and serve immediately.

Tempting Kababs

Chicken Kabab

Serves 6

Ingredients

1 ½ kg chicken

For the marinade

150 ml curd
1 onion, cut into rings
1 flake of garlic, crushed
1 tomato, sliced
1" piece of ginger, chopped
1 tsp each of coriander powder, garam
masala and red chilli powder
Juice of 1 lemon
2 tsp black pepper
Lemon wedges of garnishing
Salt to taste

Method

1. Wash and dry the chicken. Remove the meat from the bones and cut it into 2" pieces.

2. Beat the curd and mix it well with the rest of the marinade ingredients to make a smooth paste.

3. Put the chicken pieces in this mixture and leave it to marinate overnight.

4. Thread the chicken pieces onto skewers and grill for 10 minutes, until the chicken is tender.

5. Garnish with the lemon wedges, onion rings and tomato slices.

Boti Kabab

Serves 4

Ingredients

750 gm lean lamb, cut into 1" cubes
6 small onions
A few lemon wedges

For the marinade

1 tsp black pepper
½ tsp turmeric powder
1 tsp red chilli powder
150 ml curd
¼ cup oil
2 tsp coriander powder
Salt to taste

Method

1. Beat the curd and mix in the spices and salt.

2. Add the lamb cubes and leave to marinate overnight.

3. Cut the onions into quarters and separate each layer of onion.

4. Thread the onion pieces and meat alternately onto skewers. Brush with the oil. Grill for about 5-10 minutes.

5. Garnish with the lemon wedges.

Shami Kabab

Ingredients

500 gm lean lamb, cut into ½" cubes
1 small onion, grated
2 eggs, beaten
2 flakes of garlic, crushed
300 ml stock
1" piece of ginger, finely chopped
¼ tsp grated lemon rind
60 gm peas, shelled
A few coriander leaves, chopped
¼ tsp each of turmeric, red chilli
cinnamon and cumin powders
Oil for deep frying
Tomato and cucumber slices
for garnishing
Onion rings, for garnishing
Salt and pepper to taste

Method

1. Put the peas and meat along with the stock in a pan and bring to the boil. Cover and simmer until the meat is tender and the liquid is absorbed.

2. Put the meat and peas in a food processor along with the spices, salt and pepper. Process for about 2 minutes.

3. Add the ginger, garlic, onion, lemon rind and coriander leaves. Mix enough beaten egg to bind.

4. Divide the mixture into 16 balls. Roll the meat balls in the flour and deep fry them in the oil until golden brown.

5. Garnish with the onion rings, tomato and cucumber slices.

Seekh Kabab

Ingredients

500 gm minced meat
¼ tsp cardamom powder
2 onions, finely chopped
¼ tsp cumin powder
½" piece of ginger, finely chopped
¼ tsp cloves powder
2 flakes of garlic, crushed
1 tsp coriander powder
2 green chillies, chopped
1 egg, beaten
1 tbsp oil
A few coriander leaves, chopped
Salt to taste
Lemon slices for garnishing

Method

1. Mix the meat with the onions, ginger and garlic.

2. Add the spices along with salt to the meat mixture. Mix enough beaten egg to bind.

3. Divide the mixture into 8 balls. Flatten the meat balls and thread these onto the skewers.

4. Brush with the oil and place under a hot grill, turning the kababs occasionally, until the meat is cooked.

5. Garnish with the lemon slices and chopped coriander leaves.

Lamb Kabab

Serves 4-6

Ingredients

750 gm lamb
2 tsp garam masala
1 lemon
1 tsp black pepper
1 large onion
2 tsp salt
2 flakes of garlic, chopped
2 lemon wedges
2" piece of ginger, coarsely chopped
¼ cup oil
450 gm curd
4 tbsp malt vinegar
Onion rings for garnishing

Method

1. Cut the lamb into 1" cubes. Squeeze the juice of the lemon over the meat cubes, making sure that they all are well coated.

2. Chop half the onion, ginger and garlic. Add these to the curd and vinegar along with the spices. Put this mixture in a food processor and process for about 2 minutes, until it is well blended.

3. Pour this over the lamb pieces, cover and keep in the refrigerator for at least 24 hours.

4. Thread the pieces of lamb onto the skewers. Brush them with the oil.

5. Cook till the pieces are evenly done.

6. Cut the remaining onion into rings and garnish along with the lemon wedges.

Prawn Kabab

Serves 4

Ingredients

250 gm big prawns, cleaned and
deveined
2 tbsp vinegar
½ tsp garam masala
2 tbsp curd
½ tsp ground cumin
4 flakes of garlic
½ tsp coriander seeds
½" piece of ginger
2 tbsp ghee
2 tsp red chilli powder
A few drops of red food colouring
Salt to taste

Method

1. Grind the ginger and garlic to a paste.

2. Add this with the rest of the ingredients, except the ghee and prawns, to the curd. Blend well.

3. Marinate the prawns in this mixture and set aside for 2 hours.

4. Thread the prawns onto skewers, smeared with ghee and grill till golden brown in colour. Serve hot.

Fish Kabab

Serves 4

Ingredients

500 gm fish steaks
2 tbsp garam masala
½ cup curd, beaten
6 red chillies
50 gm cream
4 tbsp ghee
2 medium onions
2" piece of ginger
4 flakes of garlic
A few drops of orange food colouring
Salt to taste

Method

1. Cut the fish steaks into 1 ½" cubes.

2. Grind the onions, ginger and garlic and extract the juice.

3. Smear the juice on the fish pieces and keep aside for 30 minutes.

4. Mix the rest of the ingredients and put the fish pieces in it. Keep aside for 30 minutes more.

5. Thread the fish pieces onto skewers and grill till golden brown in colour. Serve hot.

Lotus Stem Kabab

Serves 6

Ingredients

750 gm lotus stem
3 tsp cumin powder
1 small onion, finely chopped
2 tsp garam masala
1 tsp ground ginger
¼ tsp red chilli powder
3 green chillies, chopped
60 gm roasted and ground Bengal gram
1 tbsp ghee
A few chopped coriander leaves
Salt to taste

Method

1. Scrape and cut the lotus stem into thin slices and boil in salted water till tender. Remove from the fire, cool and mash.

2. Add salt and the garam masala, ground ginger, cumin powder, coriander leaves, red chilli powder and Bengal gram. Mix well.

3. Add the chopped onions and green chillies to the lotus stem mixture.

4. With greased palms make long rolls out of this mixture and pass the skewers through them. Grill till light brown.

5. Heat 1 tbsp ghee in a frying pan and fry the seekh kababs till golden brown. Serve hot.

Spicy Fish Kabab

Serves 4-6

Ingredients

750 gm fish
¼ tsp red chilli powder
2 potatoes, cooked and mashed
2 green chillies, chopped
1 large onion, finely chopped
1 tsp freshly ground black pepper
½" piece of ginger, chopped
2 eggs, beaten
2 tbsp chopped coriander leaves
Dry breadcrumbs for coating
Lemon wedges for garnishing
Oil for deep frying
Salt to taste

Method

1. Steam the fish pieces for about 10 minutes. Cool, remove the bones from the fish and mash them.

2. Add the chopped onions and mashed potatoes. Add the green chillies, coriander leaves, ginger, chilli powder and black pepper. Sprinkle with salt. Then add one beaten egg to the mixture.

3. Divide the mixture into 8 portions. Roll into balls and then flatten them into rounds, about ½" thick.

4. Dip the kababs in the remaining beaten egg, then roll them in the dry breadcrumbs.

5. Garnish with the lemon wedges.

Bangri Kabab

Ingredients

400 gm minced meat
1 tbsp chopped green chillies
4 tbsp Bengal gram
1 tbsp chopped coriander leaves
1 tsp ginger paste
1 tsp cumin seeds
1 tsp garlic paste
4 cloves
1 onion, finely chopped
4 cardamoms
1" stick of cinnamon
¾ tsp salt
8-10 black peppercorns
Oil for frying

Method

1. Boil the minced meat with all the ingredients (except the egg, coriander leaves and green chillies) in ¾ cup water for 10-12 minutes.

2. Cook till the water evaporates.

3. Add the coriander leaves and green chillies.

4. When cool grind the mixture to a fine paste.

5. Beat the egg and add to the above mixture.

6. Divide into small portions and roll into long kababs.

7. Heat the oil in a pan and deep fry the kababs till golden brown. Serve hot and garnish with the mint leaves.

Champ Kabab

Serves 4

Ingredients

1 kg lamb chops
¼ kg curd
¼ kg onions, ground
2 tsp garlic-ginger paste
1 tsp garam masala, *freshly ground*
½ cup oil

Method

1. Wash the lamb chops. Pat dry with a clean kitchen cloth. Pierce all over with a fork.

2. Mix the onion paste, garlic-ginger paste, garam masala and curd.

3. Marinate the chops in this mix for three hours. It can also be prepared and kept overnight.

4. You can either fry the chops in oil over a medium flame or barbecue them.

5. While barbecuing, brush oil on the chops. Roast till brown.

6. Serve with mint chutney.

Chilli Kabab

Ingredients

1 kg minced meat
2 tsp black pepper
2 onions, finely sliced
12 cloves, ground
2" piece of ginger
1 tsp turmeric powder
12 green chillies, finely chopped
600 ml curd
1 bunch of coriander leaves, chopped
3 tbsp ghee
Onion rings and lemon wedges
for garnishing
Salt to taste

Method

1. Put the minced meat into a food processor and process till a fine paste is obtained.

2. Fry the sliced onions in 2 tbsp of ghee till golden brown.

3. Extract the juice from the ginger.

4. Tie the curd in a muslin cloth to drain out the liquid.

5. Pour the ginger juice into the meat paste and mix well.

6. Add the curd, pepper, salt and cloves.

7. Then add the turmeric powder, coriander leaves, chillies and browned onions to the meat.

8. Mix well and keep aside for 2 ½ hours.

9. Make small balls of the meat mixture. Keep aside for 3-4 minutes.

10. Thread the meat balls onto skewers.

11. Dip in the ghee and grill till done on all sides.

12. Serve hot garnished with the onion rings and lemon wedges.

Vegetarian Varieties

Vegetable Kofta Curry

Ingredients

375 gm potatoes
1 tbsp turmeric powder
250 gm shelled peas
1 tsp cinnamon powder
500 gm carrots
1 tsp clove powder
3 onions, coarsely chopped
¼ tsp red chilli powder
1 small pod of garlic, crushed
300 ml vegetable stock
1" piece of ginger, chopped
4 tbsp cream
2 tomatoes, pureed
A few chopped coriander leaves
Flour for coating
Oil for deep frying
Salt and pepper to taste

Method

1. Boil and mash the potatoes, peas and carrots, reserve the stock. Add salt and pepper.

2. Make small balls out of this mixture and roll them in the flour. Fry in the hot oil until golden brown.

3. Fry the onions in the ghee until golden brown. Add the ginger, garlic, turmeric, cinnamon and clove powder and a little water. Cook for 2 minutes.

4. Add the tomato puree and simmer till the gravy thickens.

5. Now add the stock, salt, pepper, chilli powder and bring to the boil.

6. Gently add the fried koftas into this gravy and simmer for 15 minutes.

7. Top the koftas with the cream and coriander leaves.

Palak Paneer

Serves 4

Ingredients

60 gm ghee
½ tsp turmeric powder
625 gm spinach
1 tsp coriander powder
½ tsp red chilli powder
½ tsp garam masala
125 gm cottage cheese, diced
1 tsp salt
1 tbsp cream

Method

1. Wash and cut the spinach. Cook it in its own moisture till dry.

2. When cool, grind the leaves in a food processor and process for 2 minutes.

3. Heat the ghee in a saucepan and add the spices and salt. Cook for 5 minutes.

4. Add the spinach paste, cover and cook over a moderate flame for 10 more minutes.

5. Add the diced cheese to the spinach paste. Cook for 5 minutes.

6. Pour the cream on top just before serving.

Palak Aloo

Ingredients

500 gm spinach
200 gm potatoes
½ tsp coriander powder
2 cardamoms
1 large onion, coarsely chopped
1 tsp black pepper
½ tsp garam masala
1 small pod of garlic, chopped
½" piece of ginger, chopped
50 gm ghee
1 tsp salt

Method

1. Wash and cut the spinach. Cook it in its own moisture till dry.

2. Peel and dice the potatoes into 1" cubes.

3. Heat the ghee in a saucepan and add the chopped onions, garlic and ginger. Then mix all the spices and cook for 2 minutes.

4. Add the potatoes and salt. Simmer for 10 minutes until they are soft.

5. Add the spinach paste and cook over a low flame till the oil separates. Keep stirring to avoid scorching.

6. Serve with roti or naan.

Tarka Dal

Serve 4-6

Ingredients

225 gm red split lentils
50 gm ghee
1 small onion, coarsely sliced
600 ml water
2 small pods of garlic, thinly sliced
1 tsp salt
2 green chillies, chopped
1 tsp cumin seeds
1 tsp turmeric
1 tbsp sesame oil

Method

1. Heat the ghee in a heavy-bottomed saucepan and fry the onion slices till soft and golden brown. Add half of the sliced garlic and cook for a few minutes.

2. Add the turmeric powder and the lentils. Then add the chillies.

3. Fry the lentils over a low flame for about a minute. Add the water and bring it to the boil.

4. Add 1 tsp salt and boil the lentils over a moderate flame until it breaks down and the mixture is thick.

5. Heat the sesame oil in a small frying pan. When it starts to smoke, add the cumin seeds and the remaining garlic. The garlic should turn brown.

6. Pour this over the lentils and serve immediately.

Palak Dal

Serves 4-6

Ingredients

225 gm red split lentils
500 gm fresh spinach
1 medium onion, finely chopped
1 tsp red chilli powder
4 flakes of garlic, sliced
½" piece of ginger, chopped
300 ml water
Salt and garam masala to taste

Method

1. Wash the lentils well and place in a heavy saucepan. Cover with the water.

2. Wash and finely chop the spinach.

3. Add the chopped onion, garlic and ginger to the lentils.

4. Cover and bring to the boil. Add the chilli powder and salt and simmer gently till the lentils are soft and a thick mixture remains.

5. Now add the spinach. Cook over a low flame till the spinach is totally mixed with the lentils.

6. Sprinkle with garam masala, stir a little and serve hot.

Aloo Bhindi Bhaji

Ingredients

225 gm ladiesfingers
1 tsp red chilli powder
225 gm potatoes
1 tsp turmeric powder
1 medium onion, sliced
1 tsp garam masala
1 tbsp chopped coriander leaves
1 tsp cumin powder
1 tsp salt
1 tsp black pepper
75 gm ghee

Method

1. Heat the ghee in a heavy saucepan and fry the sliced onions till light pink in colour.

2. Peel and slice the potatoes. Cut the ladiesfingers into ½" long pieces.

3. Add the potatoes and ladiesfinger slices to the pan.

4. Sprinkle with the spices and salt. Stir well.

5. Cover and cook over a low flame till the potatoes are done. You can pour some water if it gets very dry.

6. Serve hot, garnished with the chopped coriander leaves.

Aloo Gobi

Serves 4-6

Ingredients

1 small cauliflower
1 tsp red chilli powder
900 gm potatoes
½ tsp ground ginger
2 onions, finely sliced
2 tsp coriander powder
100 gm ghee
450 ml water
1½ tsp garam masala
Salt to taste

Method

1. Wash the cauliflower and cut into florets, trimming away any leaves. Peel and cut the potatoes into 1" cubes.

2. Heat the ghee in a large saucepan and fry the sliced onions. Add the chilli powder, ground ginger and coriander powder. Sprinkle with salt.

3. Add the potatoes and cauliflower and gently stir, so that the spices mix well.

4. Lower the flame and cook the vegetables in its own moisture.

5. Cover and cook till the vegetables are tender.

6. Add the garam masala and cook till the mixture is dry. Serve hot with naan.

Kadai Paneer

Serves 4-6

Ingredients

500 gm cottage cheese
2 tsp coriander seeds
100 gm capsicum
5 red chillies
2 green chillies, chopped
½ tsp fenugreek powder
2 tsp chopped ginger
2 tbsp chopped coriander leaves
4 tomatoes, minutely chopped
3 tbsp ghee
6 flakes of garlic, crushed to a paste
Salt to taste

Method

1. Slice the cheese and capsicum into long, thin strips.

2. Grind the coriander seeds and red chillies together.

3. Heat the ghee in a pan, add the garlic paste and chopped ginger. Fry it over a low flame for a few seconds.

4. Add the chopped tomatoes and cook till the tomatoes are tender.

5. Then add the fenugreek powder, green chillies and salt.

6. Finally add the sliced cheese and cook till the gravy is thick.

7. Garnish with the chopped coriander leaves.

Dilkhush Kofta

Ingredients

1 cup split green gram
or black gram with skin
3 tomatoes, pureed
2 tbsp cream
½ cup boiled and ground spinach
1 tsp chopped ginger
½ cup cottage cheese, crumbled
2 green chillies, chopped
½ cup gram flour
¼ tsp turmeric powder
1 tsp garam masala
2 tsp coriander powder
2 tbsp ghee
1 tsp cumin seeds
Ghee for deep frying
Salt to taste

Method

1. Soak the gram for 4 hours. Coarsely grind to a paste.

2. Mix with the spinach, salt and cheese.

3. Form 1" balls and deep fry in the hot ghee till golden brown. Keep aside.

4. In 2 tbsp ghee, fry the ginger, green chillies, turmeric and coriander powders, cumin seeds, garam masala and salt.

5. Add the tomato pulp and fry till the ghee surfaces.

6. Lower the flame, stir in the cream and ½ a cup of water and simmer till the gravy thickens.

7. Arrange the koftas in a dish and pour the hot gravy over it. Serve hot.

Khoya Makhana

Ingredients

15 cashew nuts
¼ tsp turmeric powder
100 gm khoya or thickened milk
2 tsp coriander powder
50 gm puffed lotus seeds
100 gm peas, shelled
1 tsp each of cumin seeds and sugar
3 tomatoes, sliced
*½ tsp each of dried mango and
ginger powders*
2 green chillies, chopped
Ghee for deep frying
Salt and garam masala to taste

Method

1. Roast the khoya on a hot griddle till pink.

2. In a bowl pour one cup of water and add the sugar. Boil the peas in it till soft.

3. Deep fry the cashew nuts and lotus seeds separately, drain and keep aside.

4. Heat 3 tbsp ghee in a pan.

5. Fry the cumin seeds, then add the ginger powder, green chillies, turmeric, coriander and mango powders, garam masala and salt.

6. Add the khoya, sliced tomatoes and boiled peas and cook for 5 minutes, stirring frequently.

7. Lower the flame, add half a cup of water, the fried lotus seeds and cashew nuts. Simmer for 5 minutes before removing from the fire.

Khoya-Matar Special

Serves 4-6

Ingredients

150 gm khoya, crumbled
½ tsp cumin seeds
1 ½ cups green peas, boiled
¼ tsp red chilli powder
2 onions
¼ tsp garam masala powder
2 tomatoes, pureed
2 green chillies
1" piece of ginger
2 tbsp ghee
1 cup water
A few cashew nuts
Salt to taste

Method

1. Grind the green chillies, ginger and cumin seeds to a paste. Grind the onions separately.

2. Heat the ghee in a pan. Add the onion paste and fry till light brown. Add the khoya (keeping aside a little for garnishing). Cook over a low flame till the khoya turns light brown.

3. Add the ginger-garlic paste and cook for a minute. Add the cashew nuts and saute for a minute.

4. Add the tomato puree and saute till the ghee floats on top. Add the green peas and cook for 2 to 3 minutes.

5. Add the water, red chilli and garam masala powders and salt. Cook till the gravy is thick.

6. Garnish with the grated khoya, cashew nuts and green peas. Serve hot.

Dal Makhani

Serves 4-6

Ingredients

For boiling with the gram

250 gm whole black gram
1" piece of ginger, chopped
2 red chillies
4 flakes garlic
2 pinches asafoetida
5 cups water
2 pinches soda bicarb
Salt to taste

For the gravy

4 small tomatoes, pureed
2 tsp coriander powder
1 cup milk
2 green chillies, crushed

¾ cup curd, beaten
1 tsp tandoori masala
3-4 tbsp butter
½ tsp garam masala powder
3 tbsp ghee
A few coriander leaves

Method

1. Boil the gram with all the ingredients till the gram is tender.
2. Heat the ghee in a pan, add the tomato puree and green chillies. Saute until the ghee floats on top.
3. Add ½ cup curd and coriander powder, and cook for a few seconds.
4. Add the tomato mixture to the boiled dal. Add the milk, butter, garam masala and *tandoori* masala.
5. Simmer over a low flame for about 10 minutes.
6. Top it with the remaining beaten curd and coriander leaves.

Khatte Chane

Ingredients

200 gm chickpeas
½ tsp red chilli powder
50 gm Bengal gram
1½ tsp garam masala
50 gm onions, finely chopped
2 lemons, finely sliced
100 gm tamarind
4 green chillies, chopped
2" piece of ginger, chopped
2 ⅔ cups of water
A pinch of soda bicarb
A few fresh coriander leaves
50 gm ghee
Salt to taste

Method

1. Clean, wash and soak the chickpeas and Bengal gram overnight with the soda bicarb.

2. Boil them in 2⅔ cups of water till done.

3. Soak the tamarind and extract the pulp. Reserve the liquid.

4. In a pan, heat the ghee and lightly brown the chopped onion and ginger pieces.

5. Add the tamarind water, garam masala, red chilli powder, green chilli and salt.

6. Then add the boiled chickpeas and Bengal gram. Cook over a low flame till the gravy is thick.

7. Garnish with the coriander leaves and finely sliced lemon rings.

Chana Masala

Ingredients

250 gm chickpeas
1 tbsp dry mango powder
2" piece of ginger, thinly sliced
1 tsp red chilli powder
4 green chillies
2 tsp coriander powder
200 gm ghee
2 tsp cumin powder
2 ½ cups water
4 tsp garam masala
Salt to taste

Method

1. Soak the chickpeas overnight.
2. Then boil it in water till done.
3. Strain the chickpeas and keep in a pan.
4. Mix all the ingredients with the boiled chickpeas, except the ghee.
5. Heat the ghee in a separate pan till it begins to smoke. Pour it evenly over the chickpeas.
6. Place the pan over a low flame and simmer for 10 minutes. Add 1-2 tsp of water if necessary. Serve hot.

Mughlai Aloo Kofta

Ingredients

½ kg potatoes
1 tsp garam masala
1" piece of ginger, finely chopped
1 ½ tsp cumin powder
2 tsp ground poppy seeds
2 tsp chopped coriander leaves
4 green cardamoms
100 gm flour
2 green chillies, chopped
Breadcrumbs for coating
Ghee for deep frying
Salt to taste

For the filling

180 gm cottage cheese
A pinch of yellow colour
Salt to taste

Method

1. Boil the potatoes in salted water till tender.

2. Cool, peel and grate the potatoes. Add the chopped ginger, coriander leaves and green chillies.

3. Mix well the spices with the potatoes.

4. Make a thick batter of the flour with water and keep aside.

5. Mash the cheese and then mix the yellow colour and salt.

6. Make small round balls of the cheese and cover each ball with the potato mixture.

7. Dip in the flour batter, roll in the breadcrumbs and deep fry in the ghee till golden brown. Serve hot.

Masala Baingan

Serves 4

Ingredients

2 large aubergines
1 tsp black pepper
100 gm carrots, peeled and diced
1" piece of ginger, sliced
100 gm peas
170 gm tomatoes, peeled and sliced
75 gm ghee
1 large onion, coarsely chopped
Salt to taste

Method

1. Cut the aubergines lengthwise into halves and boil in salted water for 10-15 minutes.
2. Drain the water and carefully scoop out the pulp of the aubergines so that the peel does not break. Keep the pulp aside.
3. Heat the ghee in a large frying pan and fry the chopped onions until soft. Add the peas and carrots. Fry over a low flame.
4. Mash the aubergine pulp and add to the mixture in the pan along with the tomatoes. Add the pepper, salt and stir well.
5. When the vegetables are almost cooked, add the ginger slices.
6. Arrange the aubergine halves in a baking tray and fill the cooked mixture into the peel.
7. Bake in a preheated oven at 180°C for about 25 minutes, until they are golden brown.

Shahi Paneer

Serves 4

Ingredients

250 gm cottage cheese, cut into long
strips
1 tbsp tomato sauce
4 large tomatoes, chopped
½ tsp red chilli powder
1 onion, coarsely chopped
½ tsp garam masala
1/3 cup milk or thin cream
2 black cardamoms, crushed
¼ cup curd
1 green chilli, chopped
1½ tbsp cornflour, dissolved in ½ cup
water
1" piece of ginger, crushed
3 tbsp coriander leaves, chopped
Ghee for deep frying
Salt to taste

120

Method

1. Fry the chopped onions, ginger, green chillies and black cardamoms in 2 tbsp ghee until light brown.

2. Add the tomatoes and fry for 8-10 minutes.

3. Add the curd and saute for 4-5 minutes.

4. Cool and grind to a puree with ½ cup water.

5. Strain and boil the puree.

6. Add the cornflour paste, stirring constantly.

7. Add the red chilli powder, garam masala powder and tomato sauce.

8. Add salt and cook till the gravy is thick. Keep aside.

9. Heat the ghee and deep fry the cottage cheese strips without browning them. Keep aside.

10. Just before serving, heat the gravy and add the cottage cheese pieces.
11. Add the cream or milk.
12. Garnish with the coriander leaves.

Chicken Delights

Dhania Murgh

Serves 4

Ingredients

1 medium chicken, cut into
medium-size pieces
1 tsp turmeric powder
600 ml curd
5 green chillies, slit into 2 each
250 gm khoya or thickened milk
4 tbsp ghee
600 ml coconut milk extract
2 large bunches of coriander leaves
6 flakes garlic
1 ½" piece of ginger
60 gm almonds
60 gm raisins
Salt to taste

Method

1. Grind the ginger and garlic to a paste and coat the chicken pieces with it.
2. Heat the ghee in a saucepan and fry the chicken pieces till evenly browned. Drain and keep aside.
3. Blend the curd and khoya together to a smooth paste. Mix the turmeric powder and salt. Blanch and slice the almonds.
4. Reheat the ghee and fry the almonds and raisins. Add the curd mixture and fried chicken and cook over a low flame till dry.
5. Add the slit green chillies, chopped coriander leaves and coconut milk and bring to the boil.
6. Reduce the flame and simmer without stirring till the chicken is tender and the ghee surfaces.
7. Serve hot with plain rice.

Chicken-Do-Piaza

Serves 4

Ingredients

1 medium chicken, cut into pieces
6 flakes of garlic
500 gm onions, finely sliced
6 dry red chillies
750 gm tomatoes
1" piece of ginger
8 small potatoes, finely sliced
½ tsp peppercorns
1 ½ tbsp coriander powder
½ tsp saffron dissolved in 1 tbsp hot milk
1 tbsp cumin seed powder
600 ml water
4 tbsp ghee
Salt to taste

Method

1. Grind the coriander powder, cumin powder, garlic, chillies and ginger in a grinder.

2. Peel and slice the tomatoes and potatoes.

3. Heat the ghee in a heavy saucepan and fry the onions till tender.

4. Add the ground spices, peppercorns, tomatoes and mix well. Cook till the gravy becomes thick.

5. Add the chicken and fry for 10 minutes.

6. Add the water and saffron dissolved in milk. Cover and simmer till the chicken is tender.

7. Add the potatoes and cook till the potatoes and the chicken are done. Serve hot with naan.

Shahi Pasand Chicken

Serves 4

Ingredients

*1 medium chicken, cut into
small pieces
4 green chillies, sliced
3 medium onions, sliced
½" piece of ginger, sliced
4 tbsp ghee
1 small cauliflower, cut into florets
120 gm cottage cheese, diced
60 gm shelled peas, parboiled
4 dry red chillies
100 gm chicken liver, finely sliced
1 tsp cumin seeds
2 tomatoes, halved
2 tbsp coriander leaves
60 gm black mushrooms
1 cup boiling water
Salt and pepper to taste*

Method

1. Fry the sliced onions in the ghee till golden brown.
2. Fry the chicken in the ghee. When half done, add the sliced ginger, green chillies, salt and pepper and fry for some more time.
3. Add 1 cup boiling water and simmer over a low flame till the chicken is tender. Remove the chicken from the gravy and keep on a serving plate.
4. Add the cauliflower, peas, liver, cumin seeds and red chillies to the gravy and cook for 10 minutes.
5. Add the tomatoes, mushrooms, cottage cheese and stir well. Cover and cook for 5-7 minutes.
6. Pour the gravy along with the vegetables over the chicken. Garnish with the chopped coriander leaves.

129

Palak Murgh

Serves 4

Ingredients

1 medium chicken, cut into pieces
2 onions, sliced
500 gm spinach
4 flakes of garlic, crushed
2 tomatoes, finely chopped
2 cloves
2 tbsp ghee
1 tsp coriander powder
½ tsp freshly ground black pepper
4 tbsp whipped cream
Salt to taste

Method

1. Wash and finely cut the spinach.

2. Heat the ghee in a pan and lightly fry the sliced onions and crushed garlic.

3. Add the cloves, coriander powder, pepper, chopped tomatoes and spinach and cook for 5 minutes.

4. Add the chicken pieces and salt. Cover and cook over a low flame till the chicken is tender.

5. Pour the whipped cream on top just before serving.

Chicken Korma

Serves 4

Ingredients

750 gm chicken
3 onions
300 ml curd or yogurt
1 tbsp cumin powder
1 tbsp desiccated coconut
1 tsp coriander powder
2 tbsp ghee
½ tsp turmeric powder
2 red chillies
½ tsp ground ginger
½ tsp fenugreek
2 cardamoms, crushed
A few lemon wedges
Salt to taste

Method

1. Cut the chicken into 1" pieces. Slice two of the onions thinly.

2. Heat the ghee in a large pan and fry the chillies and sliced onions.

3. Chop the remaining onion and add it to the pan along with the spices, except the cardamoms. Mix the coconut. Fry until the spices darken, but not burn, in colour.

4. Add the chicken pieces, salt, cardamoms and half of the curd. Simmer until the chicken is tender. Add a little water if the gravy gets too dry.

5. After the chicken is cooked, stir in the remaining curd.

6. Garnish with the lemon wedges and serve with plain rice.

Kaju Chicken

Ingredients

4 chicken joints
1 tsp red chilli powder
300 ml chicken stock
2 tbsp ghee
1 tbsp curry powder
2 large onions, finely chopped
300 ml curd
2 flakes of garlic, crushed
125 gm cashew nuts, chopped
1" piece of ginger, finely chopped
Salt to taste

Method

1. Put the chicken pieces in the chicken stock and simmer for about 45 minutes, till tender. Drain the chicken and keep aside. Reserve 150 ml of stock.

2. Heat the ghee in a heavy frying pan and fry the onions, garlic and ginger.

3. Add the chilli powder and curry powder and fry for some more time.

4. Beat the curd with the chicken stock and add to the onion mixture. Bring it to the boil.

5. Add the chicken and simmer for a few minutes.

6. Stir in the chopped cashew nuts and salt.

7. Serve hot with plain rice.

Kesar Murgh

Serves 4-6

Ingredients

8 chicken legs
3 tbsp oil
2 onions, finely chopped
2 flakes of garlic, crushed
½ tsp saffron strands
½ tsp ground ginger
1 tbsp boiling water
2 green chillies, seeded and chopped
Freshly ground black pepper to taste
Salt to taste

Method

1. Season the chicken with salt and pepper.

2. Soak the saffron strands in the boiling water.

3. Heat the oil in a large saucepan and fry the chicken till evenly browned. Drain the chicken and keep aside.

4. Add the onions, garlic, ginger and chillies to the remaining oil in the pan and fry over a low flame till the onions are soft and golden.

5. Stir in the saffron along with the liquid.

6. Add the chicken and stir well so that the saffron mixture coats the chicken.

7. Cook over a moderate flame till the chicken is tender. Add a little water if the gravy becomes too dry.

8. Serve hot with parathas.

Murgh Dahi

Serves 6

Ingredients

1 ½ kg chicken
4 flakes of garlic, chopped
600 ml curd
3" piece of ginger, chopped
100 gm ghee
1 tsp salt
4 green chillies, chopped
1 tsp black pepper
100 gm chopped coriander leaves

Method

1. Wash the chicken and make deep cuts on the surface, using a sharp knife.

2. Add the salt and black pepper to the curd.

3. Grind all the above ingredients alongwith the chillies, ginger, garlic in a food processor.

4. Pour this marinade over the chicken pieces. Cover and marinate overnight.

5. Heat the ghee in a heavy saucepan and put the chicken pieces into it. Fry for about a minute and then add the marinade.

6. Cover and cook over a moderate flame until the chicken is done and the marinade is absorbed.

7. Garnish with the chopped coriander leaves and serve immediately.

Shahi Murgh

Serves 6

Ingredients

1 ½ kg chicken
1 pod garlic
100 gm cooking oil
1 green chilli, chopped
1 tsp curd
1 large onion, chopped
100 gm blanched almonds, sliced
2" piece of ginger
100 gm fresh coconut, cut into thin slices
10 cardamoms
1 tbsp chopped coriander leaves
1 tsp salt
A pinch of saffron

Method

1. Wash and cut the chicken into 8 pieces.
2. Crush the garlic and rub it over the chicken. Cover and keep aside for an hour.
3. Heat the oil in a heavy saucepan and fry the chilli and onion mixture gently for a minute. Slice the ginger and add to the above mixture along with the cardamoms and cloves. Cook for 2 minutes.
4. Add the chicken pieces and cook for another 10 minutes.
5. Add the salt, curd and saffron, cover and simmer for about 45 minutes until the chicken is cooked. The gravy should be thick.
6. Before serving, add the sliced almonds and coconut slices and garnish with fresh chopped coriander leaves.

Murgh Noorjahani

Ingredients

1 medium chicken, jointed
2 medium onions
2 cups of cream
1" piece of ginger
1 ½ cups desiccated coconut
6 flakes of garlic
25 gm each of roasted cashew nuts,
almonds, walnuts, peanuts, etc.
1 tbsp each of garam masala, cumin
powder, coriander seeds and
red chilli powder
½ cup ghee
¼ tsp saffron
Edible silver foil
Salt to taste

Method

1. Mix the cream and coconut in a saucepan. Place on fire. Cook till it begins to boil. Remove from the fire and keep aside for 30 minutes. Pass this mixture through a finely meshed sieve. Keep the liquid and discard the pulp.

2. Grind together all the nuts with the ginger, garlic and onion.

3. Heat the ghee in a heavy saucepan and brown the onion. Add the chicken and fry for 5 minutes.

4. Add the coconut cream liquid and the rest of the ingredients except the silver foil and saffron.

5. Cover and cook over a low flame till the chicken is tender and the gravy is thick.

6. Mix the saffron in 1 tsp of hot milk. Pour over the dish. Decorate with the foil just before serving.

143

Mughlai Chicken

Serves 6

Ingredients

1 ½ chicken, washed and skinned
3 onions, sliced
150 ml chicken stock
½ tsp ground ginger
30 gm ground almonds
3 small pods of garlic, crushed
150 ml cream
1 tsp turmeric powder
3 tbsp oil
2 tsp garam masala
½ tsp saffron strands
A pinch of ground mace
4 tbsp hot milk
Freshly ground black pepper to taste
Salt to taste

Method

1. Cut the chicken into medium-sized pieces.

2. Coat the chicken with garlic-ginger-turmeric paste.

3. Soak the saffron in hot milk for 10 minutes.

4. Fry the onions in a large pan until golden brown.

5. Remove the onion slices and keep aside.

6. Add the chicken pieces to the same oil and cook for a few minutes.

7. Add the garam masala, mace, salt and pepper.

8. Add the stock, fried onions and saffron.

9. Cover and simmer gently till the chicken is tender.

10. Transfer the chicken pieces to the serving plate.

11. Add the almonds and cream to the gravy and heat gently, stirring constantly.

12. Pour the sauce over the chicken.

13. Serve hot with rice.

Mutton Feasts

Mirchi Gosht

Serves 4

Ingredients

750 gm mutton
3 tbsp coriander seeds
20 red chillies
6 cardamoms
10 flakes garlic, chopped
6 cloves
4" piece of ginger, chopped
2 sticks of cinnamon (2" each)
4 onions, sliced
300 ml sour curd
1 tsp turmeric powder
Juice of 1 lemon
4 tbsp ghee
A bunch of coriander leaves,
finely chopped
Salt to taste

Method

1. Wash and cut the meat into 2" cubes.

2. Heat a tsp of ghee on a griddle. Roast the red chillies. Keep aside. Fry the coriander seeds, garlic and ginger separately, using 1 tsp of ghee for each ingredient. Keep aside.

3. Heat the remaining ghee in a large saucepan and fry the onions till golden brown. Drain and keep the onions aside.

4. Fry the cloves, cardamoms, cinnamon in the ghee. Add the mutton, turmeric powder and salt. Cover and cook over a medium flame till the meat is half cooked.

5. Add the curd and fried spices and mix well. Cover and cook till the meat is tender. If necessary, add some warm water.

6. Mix in the lemon juice and fried onions just before serving. Serve hot garnished with the coriander leaves.

Mutton Korma

Serves 4

Ingredients

1 kg breast of mutton
6 large black cardamoms
10 tbsp ghee
8-10 cloves
250 gm onions, coarsely chopped
10-15 peppercorns
600 ml curd
2 tsp coriander powder
2 bay leaves
6 dry red chillies
2" piece of cinnamon
Salt to taste

Method

1. Wash and cut the mutton into 1½" pieces.

2. Heat all the ingredients in a saucepan over a low flame.

3. Stir well and add enough water to cover the mixture.

4. Cook till the meat is done, stirring occasionally.

5. The gravy should not be too thick.

6. Add a little more water, if required and cook till tender.

7. Serve hot.

Kaleji-Do-Piaza

Ingredients

1 kg mutton liver
1 tsp chilli powder
500 gm onions, finely sliced
2 tsp garam masala
500 gm tomatoes, finely sliced
150 ml curd
2 tsp turmeric powder
3 tbsp ghee
8 flakes of garlic, coarsely chopped
1 bunch coriander leaves
1" piece of ginger, coarsely chopped
4 green chillies, coarsely chopped
Salt to taste

Method

1. Wash the liver and cut into ½" cubes.

2. Heat the ghee in a saucepan. Add the onions, tomatoes, turmeric powder and fry till reddish brown.

3. Add the chopped garlic, ginger, chillies and fry for a few minutes more.

4. Add the liver pieces and fry till browned.

5. Mix the curd and cook for some more time.

6. Add the garam masala and red chilli powder and fry till the liver is tender and the ghee floats.

7. Garnish with the chopped coriander leaves.

8. Serve hot with tandoori rotis.

Masaledar Gosht

Ingredients

500 gm meat
300 ml curd
1 large onion, finely sliced
6 peppercorns
1 ½" piece of ginger, chopped
3 pieces of cinnamon
10 flakes of garlic, chopped
2 cardamoms
3 dry red chillies
4 cloves
1 tsp turmeric powder
2 tbsp ghee
Salt to taste

Method

1. Wash the meat and cut into 1½" cubes.

2. Heat the ghee in a saucepan till it smokes.

3. Add the meat and .all the other ingredients.

4. Seal the saucepan with a tight lid and cook over a low flame for about 45 minutes. There is no need to add water.

5. Unseal the saucepan, add more ghee and fry uncovered, till the meat is tender and reddish brown in colour.

6. Serve hot.

Mughlai Lamb Chops

Serves 4

Ingredients

8 lamb chops
8 flakes of garlic
2 medium potatoes
150 ml lemon juice
2" piece of ginger
2 medium onions, sliced
6 red chillies
1 tsp turmeric powder
8 tbsp ghee
Salt to taste

Method

1. Grind the ginger, garlic, chillies and turmeric powder to a paste. Mix the lemon juice and salt.

2. Pound the lamb chops gently to shape and soften them. Add the above paste to it and marinate for a few hours.

3. Heat about 8 tbsp of ghee in a deep frying pan and fry the chops until brown. Drain and keep aside.

4. Parboil the potatoes and slice them in rounds. Fry the potato slices in the remaining ghee in the frying pan.

5. Add the chops and fry over a low flame for a few minutes.

6. Fry the sliced onions in the same ghee and garnish the chops and potatoes with them before serving.

Adrakh Ghost

Ingredients

500 gm lean lamb
1 onion, finely chopped
1" piece of ginger, chopped
1 tbsp desiccated coconut
2 tsp vinegar
1 tbsp tomato puree
1 tbsp curry powder
1 tbsp oil
Salt and pepper to taste

Method

1. Fry the chopped onions in oil till golden brown.

2. Add the curry powder and cook for 2 minutes.

3. Add the meat and brown lightly.

4. Mix the tomato puree, chopped ginger, salt and pepper. Stir well, cover and let it simmer.

5. Stir occasionally and cook for about an hour.

6. When the meat is tender, garnish with the coconut and serve with rice.

Other Titles in the Series

All You Wanted To Know About

- *Soups*
- *Barbeque*
- *Chocolate*
- *Mughlai*
- *Potato*
- *Salads*
- *Meat*
- *Chinese*
- *Dessert*
- *Pasta*
- *Cakes*
- *Seafood*

Vegetarian

- *Puddings & Desserts*
- *Low Calorie Cooking*
- *Delightful Soups*
- *Kebabs & Snacks*
- *Cuisines from the World*
- *Menus from the World*

For further information contact:
STERLING PUBLISHERS PVT. LTD.
A-59 Okhla Industrial Area, Phase-II,
New Delhi- 110020.
Tel: 26387070, 26386209
E-mail: ghai@nde.vsnl.net.in